MONA

LEONARDO DA VINCI

LISA

→

This book is dedicated to the memory of my dad, Abe Rovin,
who always believed in me and my writing dreams!
This book is also dedicated to my masterpieces—my sons, Griffin and Chase,
who were introduced to art and museums at a very, very young age.
—Debbie

For Rosemary and Shirley,
for showing me that the world is full of beauty.
—Jen

SLEEPING BEAR PRESS™

Names: Rovin-Murphy, Deborah, author. | Bricking, Jennifer, illustrator.
Title: Jackie and the Mona Lisa / written by Debbie Rovin Murphy ; illustrated by Jen Bricking.
Description: Ann Arbor, MI : Sleeping Bear Press, [2022] | Audience: Ages 6-10 |
Summary: "Jackie Kennedy loved the arts. And America loved
Jackie. The first lady knew she had the country's attention and she
wanted to encourage Americans to appreciate art. This is the
little-known story about how Jackie Kennedy brought the world's most
famous painting, the Mona Lisa, to the United States"— Provided by publisher.
Identifiers: LCCN 2021046794 | ISBN 9781534111172 (hardcover)
Subjects: LCSH: Leonardo, da Vinci, 1452-1519. Mona
Lisa–Exhibitions–Juvenile literature. | Onassis, Jacqueline Kennedy,
1929-1994–Anecdotes–Juvenile literature.
Classification: LCC ND623.L5 R86 2022 | DDC 759.5–dc23/eng/20211202
LC record available at https://lccn.loc.gov/2021046794

Page 36 and 37 photos: Jackie Kennedy (https://commons.wikimedia.org/wiki/File:Mrs._Kennedy_in_the_Diplomatic_Reception_Room.jpg)
Reception Photo (Robert Knudsen White House Photographs, 1/20/1961 - 12/19/1963, Collection: White House Photographs, 12/19/1960 - 3/11/1964)
Mona Lisa (https://commons.wikimedia.org/wiki/File:Mona_Lisa,_by_Leonardo_da_Vinci,_from_C2RMF_retouched.jpg)

Jackie and the Mona Lisa

Debbie Rovin Murphy

Illustrated by Jen Bricking

PUBLISHED *by* SLEEPING BEAR PRESS™

Jackie Kennedy loved poetry.

She loved dance and music.
And she loved art!

In 1961, Jackie became the First Lady
of the United States.

And everyone loved Jackie.

More than that, everyone wanted to *be* just like her.

When Jackie wore a pillbox hat,
everyone wore a pillbox hat.

When Jackie pulled on her long white gloves,
everyone clamored for a pair.

From pearls to bows to brightly colored dresses
(for Jackie, fashion was art too), when Jackie wore a new style,
everyone wanted something just like it.

People even started cooking French food and taking French lessons—just because Jackie loved everything French.

Everyone was impressed with their new First Lady who spoke three different languages, had a college degree, and had even been a newspaper reporter.

Jackie knew she had America's attention and, more than anything, she wanted people to love art as much as she did.

So she started with her house. The White House.

The first time eleven-year-old Jackie visited
the White House, she wasn't very impressed.

Drab curtains.
Boring furniture.
And no guidebook to teach visitors about the most famous house in America.

The next time Jackie visited the White House, she was the First Lady. But the White House looked the same.

Drab curtains.
Boring furniture . . .
and still no guidebook!

Where were the pieces that told the stories of the important people who had lived there? Where were all the paintings? The antique furniture? The White House was supposed to be a symbol of American history, but the rooms weren't historical at all.

So Jackie went hunting for White House artifacts.
She dug through the White House basement.
She searched old government warehouses.
She hired experts on books, furniture, and paintings.

She filled her new home with Teddy Roosevelt's rugs, James Monroe's gilded armchairs, and portraits of Benjamin Franklin and Thomas Jefferson.

Jackie wanted to make the White House "a living museum" where Americans could visit and learn about the nation's history. So she had the White House officially declared a museum. Jackie even designed its guidebook!

On February 14, 1962, 56 million Americans turned on their televisions to watch Jackie show everyone the restored White House she had filled with American art and historical treasures.

But Jackie didn't stop there.

In the past, presidents invited world leaders to the White House. But Jackie and the President invited all kinds of artists, too—musicians, painters, actors, dancers, opera singers, and poets.

Ballerinas danced on the South Lawn.

Actors performed Shakespeare on the ballroom stage.

Violin, cello, and piano notes filled the air in the East Room.

Jackie was showing the whole world that America had inspiring art and culture.

But it wasn't enough to showcase art in the White House;
she wanted people to see art in person. She wanted more Americans
to visit museums, attend the theater, and listen to symphonies.
She wanted them to be inspired by it the same way she was.

Jackie had a plan. . . .
She would bring the world's most famous painting to America.

The *Mona Lisa*!
Jackie knew people would come to see the *Mona Lisa*.

It wasn't easy. Just the year before, Jackie and the President had visited France. Jackie enchanted the French President and his ministers with her fluent French and art expertise. Would France be willing to loan *Mona Lisa* to America?

The painting hung in a museum in Paris. And Jackie invited the man in charge of the country's art treasures, André Malraux, to Washington, D.C. Jackie told him her idea. . . .

And he agreed!

The French people did not!

"She's too fragile," cried museum officials.

"What if something happens to her?"
fumed French citizens.

"This art treasure
CANNOT travel!"
argued art experts.

But after all of the worrying and arguing and grumbling, France finally agreed to a special loan to the First Lady and President.

The *Mona Lisa* was coming to America.

And Americans couldn't wait!

The *Mona Lisa* was over 450 years old and protecting her was important.
Transporting her to America would not be an easy job. The painting
was on wood, so the temperature and humidity needed to be just right.
It was decided that the painting would travel by ship, the SS *France*.

The *Mona Lisa* was placed in a bulletproof and waterproof container that could
even float if the ship sank! Once aboard the luxury passenger ship, it was bolted
to the floor of a private cabin with a guard standing watch around the clock.

Shhh . . . she was supposed to be a secret. But when passengers found out, they were so excited, they threw a *Mona Lisa* costume party!

Two days into the voyage, the SS *France* hit rough seas and high winds.
Communication was lost. People panicked in France.
People panicked in America.
After several scary hours, the captain radioed in. *Mona Lisa* was safe!

The ship sailed into New York Harbor. Fireboats sprayed fountains of water to celebrate the *Mona Lisa*'s arrival. Police and photographers and crowds of excited people watched. Men whisked the painting off the ship and placed it into a special truck. A secret service agent was locked inside with her. Police escorted the truck all the way to Washington, D.C.

FRANCE

Jackie officially welcomed *Mona* to Washington by hosting a party of 2,000 people. The whole event was broadcast to Americans on television. Jackie's dream of introducing the most famous painting in the world to America was coming true. She couldn't wait for the *Mona Lisa* to go on display to the public.

When the big day came, long lines of people stretched down the icy streets of the Capital. They waited for hours in the frigid January cold. Old and young people, rich and poor people stood bundled up in line for their chance to see the *Mona Lisa* at Washington's National Gallery of Art. For some, this was their first visit ever to an art museum. Jackie was thrilled.

One boy hid his puppy inside his coat to give it a peek at the famous painting.

A great-grandmother waited all day in line. Twice.

People from South Carolina flew in on a plane with a picture of *Mona Lisa* on the side.

In the first hour, 3,000 people viewed the painting. (The museum usually got 3,000 visitors . . . in a whole week!)

MONA
LEONARDO DA VINCI
LISA
→

Day two brought 28,000 visitors.

By the end of the exhibit, half a million people had gotten a chance to see the famous *Mona Lisa*.

Everyone was talking about the *Mona Lisa*!

Magazines showed models wearing "Mona Lisa" haircuts.

Restaurants served special food and drinks dedicated to the painting.

The *Mona Lisa* had many fans. She even received love letters! Her face was everywhere.

Mona Lisa's next stop was the Metropolitan Museum of Art in New York City. And she was met with the same *Mona Lisa* mania.

MONA LISA

MONA LISA
LEONARDO DA VINCI
→

One million people came to see the *Mona Lisa* in New York! But the best part was that they stayed to explore the rest of the museum's art too.